Science in Ancient China

相稽

George Beshore

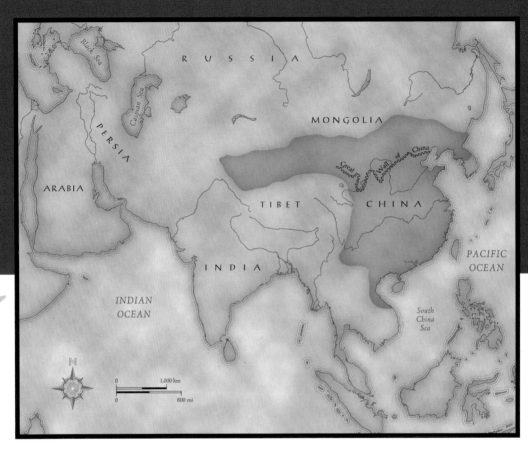

Science in Ancient China

George Beshore

相稽

Science of the Past

FRANKLIN WATTS

A Division of Grolier Publishing
New York • London • Hong Kong • Sydney
Danbury, Connecticut

Photographs ©: Ancient Art & Architecture Collection: cover, 25, 54, 10, 23 (Ronald Sheridan); Art Resource: 8, 53, 9, 12, 18 (Giraudon), 6 (Erich Lessing); E.T. Archive: 29, 31, 46; E.T.C. Wener Chinese Weapons, Royal Asiatic Society.: 19; Folio, Inc.: 30 (Fred J. Maroon); NASA: 37, 52; National Library of Medicine: 26; Paul Silverman: 50; Photo Researchers: 17, 32 (Barney Magrath/SPL), 51 (John Reader/SPL); Richard Megna: 47; Science & Society Picture Library: 22; Science and Civilization in China: 34; Superstock, Inc.: 24, 39; The Bridgeman Art Library: 35; Tony Stone Images: 27, 40 (James Balog), 28 (Zigy Kaluzny), 14 (Moggy); University of California, Lick Observatory: 38; UPI/Corbis-Bettmann: 7, 15, 16, 20, 33, 42, 55, 56; Victoria & Albert Museum: 21.

Maps created by XNR Productions Inc.

Illustrations by Drew Brook Cormack Associates

Library of Congress Cataloging-in-Publication Data

Beshore, George.
Science in ancient China / George Beshore. — Rev. ed.
p.   cm. — (Science of the past)
Includes bibliographical references and index.
Summary: Surveys the achievements of the ancient Chinese in science, medicine, astronomy, and cosmology, and describes such innovations as rockets and the compass.
ISBN 0-531-11334-5 (lib. bdg.)   0-531-15914-0 (pbk.)
1. Science—China—History—Juvenile literature. 2. Discoveries in science—China—History—Juvenile literature. 3. Engineering—China—History—Juvenile literature. 4. Science, Ancient—Juvenile literature. [1. Science—China—History. 2. Technology—China—History. 3. Inventions—China—History. 4. Science, Ancient.] I. Title. II. Series.
Q127.C5B475   1998
509'.51—dc21   97-3519
                                                                            CIP
                                                                            AC

CONTENTS

chapter 1
Wonders of Ancient Chinese Science

The original copy of this idol in the form of Marco Polo is on display at the Temple of the Five Hundred Genii in Canton, China.

When an Italian explorer named Marco Polo visited China in 1275, he was amazed by what he found. He saw rockets being shot into the air, beautiful garments made of silk, unusual medical treatments, and a strange instrument that could be used to help travelers find their way across vast deserts and wide oceans.

At a time when many Europeans lived in tiny villages connected by muddy roads, Chinese people lived in great walled cities that were connected by wide, paved roads. Everywhere Marco Polo went he found evidence of a civilization far more technically advanced than his own.

Marco Polo meeting Emperor Kublai Khan

The wonders he saw all about him were the result of centuries devoted to the study of astronomy, math, medicine, engineering, alchemy, biology, and physics. The Chinese people had been using science and technology since ancient times to improve their way of life.

Origins of a Great Civilization

Early humans lived in northern China more than 500,000 years ago. Stone tools found by modern researchers show that Chinese civilization began to develop in the rich river valleys of eastern Asia more than 7,000 years ago.

Ancient Chinese legends say that early rulers taught the people in the Yellow River Valley to grow crops and govern themselves about 5,000 years ago. This was about the same time that the ancient Egyptians were building the Great Pyramid in the Valley of the Nile. The same Chinese legends say that, during the next several centuries, other mythical rulers showed their people how to domesticate animals and raise silkworms.

Because the Chinese wanted to keep records, they developed a system of writing about 3,500 years ago. At first they scratched short messages on animal bones. The symbols they used eventually evolved into

A Chinese scribe recorded information on this bone more than 3,500 years ago.

8

the written language they use today. Chinese is the oldest, continuously used written language in the world.

As time passed, the Chinese Empire spread. Long before the birth of Christ, the Chinese ruled an area larger than the eastern half of the United States. To control such a vast area, the Chinese linked their cities with paved roads that often cut through mountains and crossed rushing rivers. More than 3,000 years ago, Chinese rulers regularly sent messages to and received information from frontier regions more than 1,000 miles (1,500 km) from the capital city. Such communications were unheard of in Europe.

Early Chinese farmers were able to raise more than enough of crops to feed themselves, so their civilization developed. Other people could spend their time building great cities, producing art and music, and studying the world around them. Because towering mountains and harsh deserts separated China from other developing cultures, many of their early ideas about the world are very different from the Western philosophies that originated in Egypt, Greece, and Rome.

Emperor Wudi receiving a letter

The Chinese View of the World

About 3,000 years ago, Chinese philosophers thought everything in the world was made up of five elements: wood, fire, earth, metal, and water. They thought they could explain all the changes that take place in nature in terms of the five elements.

They saw that wood undergoes a basic change to produce a fire's flames and that fire changes wood to ashes, which was considered a form of earth. Because metals such as iron are mined from the ground, they thought that these metals are produced by earth and that metal produces water because dew collects on metal surfaces during the night. The circular relationship

Taoist sages admire a painting of a yin-yang symbol

between the five elements was completed when water provided plants, including trees, with the moisture and nutrients they need to grow.

The Chinese also viewed the world and everything in it as a balance between two basic forces called *yin* and *yang*. Yin was related to femininity and intuitive ways of thinking. It influenced cold, wet, and passive substances. Yang was linked to masculinity and the intellectual side of males and females. It influenced warm, dry, active substances. The sun, which produces light and heat, and daytime in general were associated with yang. Night and the moon, which reflects the sun's light, were associated with yin.

According to Chinese philosophers, everything contained both yin and yang, but, in most cases, one force was dominant. Thus, yin and yang were considered to be different parts of a single overall force. This universal force was called *Tao* (pronounced DOW).

Tao is usually translated as "the way" or "the path." It is the course that all things follow when they are in tune with nature. One of the goals of ancient Chinese science was to discover the Tao of objects or ideas, or better yet, to find the Tao of nature as a whole.

Contact with Other Cultures

The Chinese considered their way of life so superior to that of other cultures that they had no desire to visit or trade with foreign lands. As a result, their civilization developed in relative isolation and they kept most of their ideas and knowledge to themselves.

Finally, around 1,900 years ago, a Chinese explorer named Zhang Qian set out on a long westward journey. He went as far west as what is now

Incredible Insects

Because the Chinese had a Taoist view of the world, they felt close to nature and all living creatures. Perhaps this is why they were the first culture to use natural *pesticides*. Instead of developing toxic chemical poisons, Chinese farmers looked to nature for ways to destroy insects and other pests that threatened their crops.

According to a Chinese manuscript written about 1,700 years ago, farmers in southern China bought small bags of ants at central markets. When they hung the bags in orange groves, the ants spread out and fed on the mites and spiders that threatened the orange crop.

The Chinese have been using silk to make beautiful garments for thousands of years.

The Chinese also found a good use for another insect—the silkworm. No one knows exactly when the Chinese first learned to raise silkworms and weave a fine cloth from the fine threads that make up a silkworm's cocoon. But we do know that silk production has flourished in the Yellow River Valley for more than 4,000 years.

A silkworm's cocoon consists of a single strand of silk that may be up to 3,000 feet (900 m) long. Unwinding a cocoon without breaking the silk thread is a great challenge. To make it easier, each cocoon is soaked in hot water to loosen the sticky material that holds it together. Women usually unwound the cocoons, but men often helped to weave the thread into cloth.

Afghanistan. From there, he sent out small groups. Some traveled south to the Persian Gulf, while others traveled to areas including what are now Iran and Russia. Qian introduced Chinese ideas to the West and brought information about other cultures back to China.

The Europeans who heard about the Chinese civilization were eager to obtain fine silks, porcelain, and other products from China. They began to make long journeys across the tall mountains and blazing deserts of Central Asia. Because the trip was so difficult, contact between the East and West was limited for the next 1,000 years.

Then, in the late 1200s, Marco Polo made his famous journey to the Orient. When he returned, Polo wrote a book called *Description of the World*. As Europeans read the book, knowledge of China's wonderful products and amazing discoveries spread quickly.

chapter 2
Secrets of Alchemy

Alchemists experimented with a
variety of ingredients in an effort to
create an elixir of life.

The roots of modern chemistry can be traced back to early China. The science of *alchemy* began as a search for the answer to an age-old question: What makes life on Earth possible? Early alchemists believed that if they mixed just the right combination of materials together, they could create a magical potion that would cure every type of human disease and allow people to live longer—perhaps forever. Alchemists were also looking for a way to change common metals into gold.

Alchemists used symbols such as dragons to represent chemical processes.

This Chinese alchemist is smoking a pipe while crushing materials with a foot grinder.

Forever Young

Alchemists thought they could bring about basic changes within people's bodies. The alchemists tried to create an *elixir of life* that would cure all human diseases, extend life, restore youth, and increase the physical and mental powers of anyone who drank it.

Many of the mixtures alchemists created made people feel better because they contained alcohol or other drugs that gave the user a temporary lift. Arsenic was a popular ingredient in elixirs. In small quantities, arsenic produces a temporary feeling of well-being. The alchemists thought that if a little arsenic was good, then a lot of arsenic would be great. Unfortunately, arsenic is extremely poisonous. There is no way of knowing how many people were accidentally killed by the alchemists' experimental potions.

Some alchemists were women. Among them was Kêng Hsien-Seng, who lived in the 800s. She was so well respected that she was summoned to court by the emperor. She told fortunes, performed magic, and experimented with elixirs of life. Li Shao-Yum lived in the 1100s. She dressed in Taoist robes and wandered across south-central China. Along the way, she prepared elixirs, recited poetry, and told fortunes.

Going for the Gold

Many early alchemists were more interested making a fortune than in creating a potion that would make them live forever. But while some of them were only interested in cheating rulers and rich people, others honestly thought they could transform common metals into gold. Based on what the alchemists saw in the world around them, it seemed possible to change one metal into another.

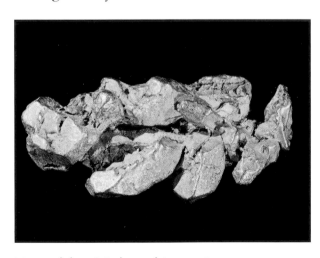

And, in some cases, the alchemists were successful. They found that by mixing copper and tin—two soft metals—they could create a hard substance called bronze. The Chinese used

Many alchemists hoped to create gold from inexpensive materials.

This bronze wine vase is more than 3,000 years old.

bronze to make strong swords, spears, and shields. Bronze was also fashioned into fine vases and figurines. Today, in the Olympic games, third-place medals are made of bronze.

Alchemists also made brass by combining zinc carbonate and copper. Because brass and gold are both shiny and similar in color, the Chinese thought they were just a few steps away from creating gold. By adding arsenic to a variety of metals, the alchemists made materials that resembled silver and gold. And iron was hardened into steel by heating it in charcoal. Despite all these useful discoveries, the alchemists were never able to find a way to make gold.

The ancient Chinese used gunpowder to launch flaming arrows toward their enemies.

The Gunpowder Explosion

Although alchemists never accomplished their main goals, they did make many important discoveries. For example, when they mixed charcoal, saltpeter, and sulfur, they created a black powder that changed the course of history. At the time, no one dreamed that this substance would one day be used to blow up buildings and shoot bullets through the air.

It did not take long for people to figure out ways to use the explosive black mixture. In the 900s, the Chinese used it during battle to launch flaming arrows against enemies. They also

The world's first cannon had barrels made of bamboo. Rocks and iron were launched by a gunpowder explosion.

packed it into grenade-like bombs, which they threw at enemy troops. In the 1200s, they developed a kind of cannon made of hollow bamboo tubes. They filled the tubes with the black powder, rocks, and pieces of iron. When this material was ignited, an explosion occurred and the rock and iron were thrust toward the enemy. Soon, news of this magical mixture spread to the Middle East and then to Europe.

It did not take long for Europeans to understand how this powerful black substance, which is now known as gunpowder, could change the way wars were fought. They began to build weapons of their own. First came muskets and rifles, then pistols, and, eventually, machine guns.

In the meantime, the Chinese continued to build more and more sophisticated weapons. By the late 1300s, they developed two-stage rockets.

The first stage carried a "warhead" up over an advancing army, then the second stage released a hail of arrows that rained down on the enemy troops.

The Ultimate Tool for Navigation

About 2,800 years ago, Chinese alchemists noticed that some rocks had a very mysterious property. These *lodestones* were able to attract a variety of metals. By studying these rocks, the Chinese learned that they all contained a type of iron ore called *magnetite*. That's why the lodestone's attractive force is called *magnetism* today.

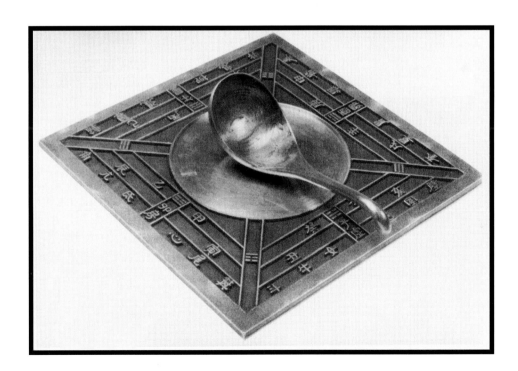

The oldest known compass has a spoon made of magnetite and a base made of bronze.

This compass was used by Chinese sailors.

The Chinese discovered that a spoon-shaped piece of lodestone always points in the same direction. Within a few centuries, the Chinese had found a way to use lodestone. They embedded the magnetic rocks into wooden blocks carved in the shape of fish. On overcast days, sailors placed these wooden fish in the water to help them figure out which way to sail. Chinese army commanders used these primitive compasses, too.

About 1,300 years ago, the Chinese learned that rubbing a steel needle on a lodestone made the needle magnetic too. Soon they began making compasses that had a magnetized needle. Eventually, Chinese builders used compasses to make straight roads. And Chinese explorers relied on compasses to find their way across stormy seas, tall mountains, and blazing deserts.

The Origin of Fine China and Herbal Remedies

Besides inventing the processes for making brass, bronze, and steel, the ancient Chinese developed a technique for firing clay to make *porcelain.* This is why porcelain is often called "fine China" today. The Chinese method, which was perfected by the 900s, produced an incredible variety of porcelain vases, urns, and dishes that are still considered to be among the finest in the world.

The ancient Chinese also learned about the chemical properties of herbs that could be used for cooking or as powerful medications.

At one time, this porcelain drug jar was used to store an elixir applied to bruises.

chapter 3
Medicine in Ancient China

Ancient Chinese herbalists prepared remedies from a wide variety of ingredients.

In China's earliest days, medical knowledge was passed from one person to another. Thanks to the work of alchemists, Chinese healers had a variety of drugs at their disposal. They used plants to ease pain, reduce fever, and treat colds. A book written about 1,500 years ago by a doctor named T'ao Hung Ching describes close to 730 medical uses for plants.

While the study of alchemy made its mark on ancient Chinese medicine, knowledge of herbs and other plants is just one small part of what Chinese doctors knew about the human body and healing. As medical knowledge increased, the Chinese Empire decided to establish a procedure for examining and licensing doctors. Then, around 1,100 years ago, Chinese doctors began to attend medical school.

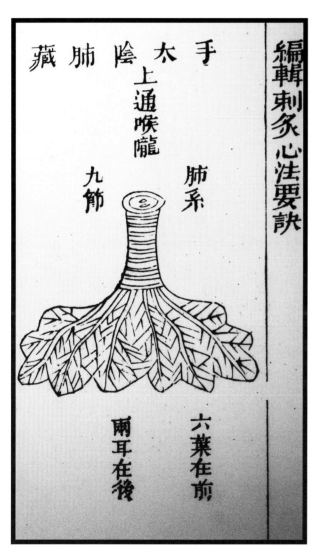

Recipes for herbal medications were recorded by early Chinese physicians such as T'ao Hung Ching.

More than 4,000 years ago, the Chinese developed herbal cures for a variety of ailments.

Acupuncture and Moxa

The roots of Chinese medicine can be traced back more than 4,000 years to a mythical emperor named Huang-Ti. Because Chinese philosophers saw everything in terms of two opposing forces—yin and yang, they believed that pain and illness occurred when the balance between these two forces was somehow disrupted. Chinese doctors believed that it was their job to restore the balance between yin and yang in their patients' bodies.

One of the earliest treatments developed by Chinese healers is called *acupuncture*. During this procedure, a trained professional sticks thin, sharp needles into specific points along the patient's body. Although bone needles were used initially, the Chinese switched to metal ones when they learned to use bronze and copper. Skilled acupuncturists knew how to insert the needles in a way that caused little or no pain.

The ancient Chinese believed that acupuncture affected the flow of *ch'i,* a life force that flows through the body. The energy of ch'i was thought to be related to the Tao force.

They used acupuncture to treat acute diseases, the kind that strike quickly and reach a crisis immediately.

Acupuncture is still used today to relieve arthritis, asthma, migraines, ulcers, and eye diseases. During the last 20 years, acupuncture has become more widely accepted in the United States, though doctors are not sure how it works. Some people believe the needles temporarily interrupt the transmission of pain messages through the nervous system.

Acupuncture doll with pins

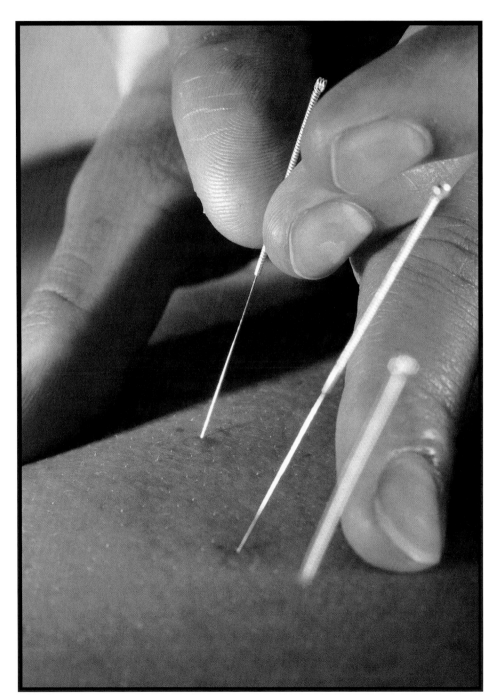

Today, acupuncture is used to relieve pain and tension in patients living all over the world.

In ancient China, country doctors often performed moxibustion on patients.

Early Chinese healers also practiced *moxa,* sometimes called *moxibustion.* In this treatment, specific sites along the body were stimulated by heat rather than needles. Small cones, dried leaves, or sticks of wormwood plants were placed at various sites along the body and set on fire. The ashes were rubbed into the blisters that formed on the patient's skin.

The Chinese used this procedure to treat chronic, or long-lasting, illnesses. The procedure was also used in Europe during the 1600s and 1700s to treat epilepsy, lower-back pain, stroke, insanity, and blindness.

Blood Circulation

Just as the Tao had two opposing forces—yin and yang, ch'i could be separated into two parts. As the Chinese looked for clues to how the life force moved through the body, they discovered how blood flows.

The earliest evidence of their knowledge about the *circulatory system* comes from a book written around the year 100. The yin-ch'i was said to circulate inside the blood vessels,

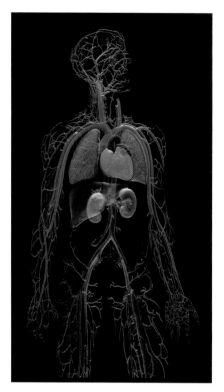

In this model of the human circulatory system, red represents arteries and blue indicates veins.

while the yang-ch'i moved outside them. A couple of centuries later, the Chinese claimed that the motion of the ch'i depends on the circulation of the blood, which flows continuously in one direction and stops only when a person dies. These statements were recorded more than 1,500 years before English physician William Harvey "discovered" how blood circulates through the body.

Once the Chinese understood how blood flows, they began to develop surgical techniques. Around the year 200, they invented a type of wine that produced *anesthesia* in patients. This enabled them to perform types of surgery that were not even attempted in Europe until the 1800s.

Conquering Disease-causing Pests

In many ways, Chinese medicine was hundreds of years ahead of Western medicine. Although the Chinese did not really understand how infections spread from one person to another, they developed a number of ways to stop viruses, bacteria, and other disease-causing agents from spreading.

More than 2,000 years ago, the Chinese began to use "fire treatment" to prevent the spread of disease. When someone died of an infectious disease, the Chinese cleansed the individual's home by burning a chemical that gives off poisonous smoke. This is the first known example of *disinfecting* an area by destroying germs.

During an epidemic in 980, a Chinese monk named Tsan-Ning advised people to steam the clothes of sick people, so that other family members would not become ill. This was the first use of *antiseptics,* a compound or process that prevents the growth of germs. Antiseptic methods were not routinely used in Western hospitals for another 900 years.

By the year 1000, the Chinese had developed a *vaccination* that prevented people from becoming infected by the virus that causes smallpox. Not until 1796 did an English physician named Edward Jenner discover a way to protect people against this deadly disease.

Edward Jenner injecting a child with a vaccination against the smallpox virus

31

chapter 4
Searching the Skies

Ancient Chinese astrologers and
astronomers were fascinated by the
star-filled night sky.

At the same time that alchemists were searching for the meaning of life and healers were developing medical techniques, other Chinese scientists were scanning the night sky. Some were *astrologers* who thought they could predict the future by plotting the movements of the stars. Others were *astronomers* who carefully measured the orbits of planets.

Observatories and Instruments

According to legend, the first astronomical observatories in China were built more than 4,000 years ago by Emperor Huang-Ti. He is also credited with teaching people how to write, play music, and raise silkworms. By 2,500 years ago, Chinese stargazers had cataloged 1,464 stars and grouped them into patterns called *constellations.*

Emperor Huang-Ti

The Chinese used a vertical pole, called a *gnomon,* to measure changes in the length of the sun's shadow over weeks and months. They noticed that the shadow grew longer and longer until around December 22. At this time, the sun is farthest from the North Pole and people living in the Northern Hemisphere experience the shortest day and longest night of the year. Today, scientists call this the *winter solstice.*

Following the winter solstice, the shadow becomes shorter and shorter until around June 22. At the *summer solstice,* the sun is closest to the North Pole, so people in the Northern Hemisphere experience the longest day and the shortest night of the year.

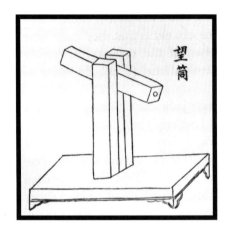

In ancient China, stargazers used a sighting tube to look at faint stars.

Another instrument was used to view very faint stars. Unlike a modern telescope, which has lenses, this was a simple tubelike tool. It shut out other sources of light, allowing the Chinese to concentrate on a single object in the night sky. The tube helped stargazers track stars and planets and accurately predict their position above the horizon.

Chinese Calendars

The earliest Chinese stargazers learned the relationship between certain constellations and events on Earth. As a result, they were able to predict tides and seasonal changes. A priest or king who knew when spring floods would occur and could tell farmers when to plants their crops seemed to possess godlike powers. His subjects worshipped him and obeyed his commands.

34

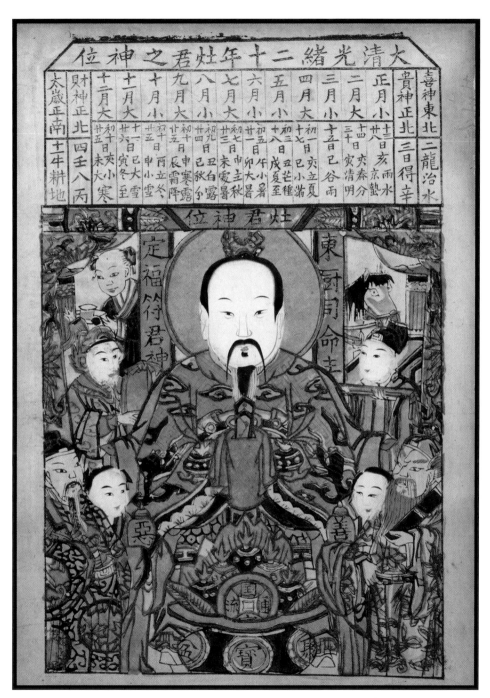

A lunar calendar
with a painting
of the Chinese
kitchen god

Eventually, the Chinese began to develop calendars to predict the seasons. Records from more than 3,500 years ago show that the Chinese believed that a year was 365¼ days long. This is amazingly close to the actual length of a year—365.24219 days. (A year is the length of time it takes for Earth to circle the sun once.)

Documents from about 3,200 years ago show that astronomers divided the Chinese year into twelve *lunar months*. A lunar month is the length of time it takes for the moon to circle Earth once. The Chinese lunar month was 29.53 days long. This, too, is surprisingly close to the actual length of a lunar cycle—29.530879 days. Because the Chinese year consisted of twelve lunar months, it had approximately 360 days. Since a year is actually a little more than 365 days long, the emperor added an extra month to the calendar from time to time.

Eclipses, Novas, Sunspots, and Comets

Thousands of years ago, Chinese astronomers were observing and recording events that occurred in space. They described an *eclipse* of the moon that took place about 3,350 years ago and an eclipse of the sun that occurred about 3,220 years ago. After that, they began to keep regular records of eclipses. By 3,000 years ago, the Chinese were able to predict an eclipse of the sun or the moon. Western astronomers did not learn to predict eclipses accurately for another 500 years.

Chinese astronomers also noticed that unusual stars sometimes appeared suddenly, burned brightly for a short time, and then disappeared. The first recorded sighting of such a "guest star" was about 3,300

During a solar eclipse, the moon moves between the sun and Earth.

years ago. It seemed to be near a star that is now called Antares and was visible for only 2 days. Today these "guest stars" are called *novas*. A nova is a star whose brightness suddenly increases tremendously and then gradually fades. Modern astronomers spot dozens of novas every year.

Once every century or two a star explodes, rather than slowly burning out. This event is called a *supernova*. The first documented supernova explosion occurred in June of 1054 when a star in the constellation Taurus suddenly flared up. Chinese observers reported that it was as bright as Venus. The supernova could be seen during daylight hours and

When a star explodes,
the result is a bright
supernova. Even
hundreds of years
later, a cloud of gas
and dust—a nebula—
still remains.

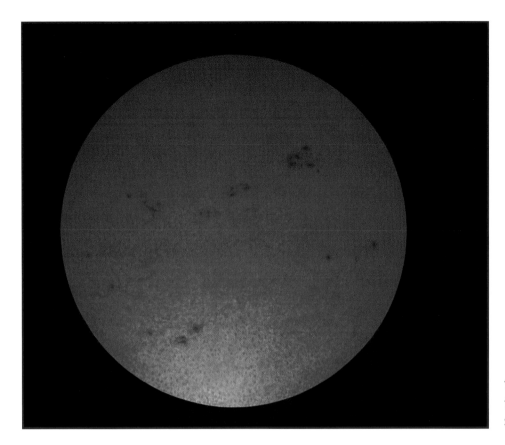

The dark areas on this image of the sun are sunspots.

sent out reddish-white flares that were visible for 23 days. The remnant of this explosion—a huge cloud of gas and dust called the Crab Nebula—can still be seen today.

About 2,000 years ago, the Chinese began to notice dark spots on the surface of the sun. They thought these blotches were shadows cast by flying birds. Today we know that these sunspots, which usually last for about a week, are cooler than surrounding regions of the sun's surface. The smallest sunspots are about as wide as the distance from Boston,

Massachusetts, to Richmond, Virginia. Some sunspots are several times larger than Earth.

The Chinese knew it is not wise to look directly at the sun when observing an eclipse or sunspots. They viewed these phenomena through translucent rock crystals or transparent jade.

The Chinese also studied passing *comets*. A comet is a ball of ice that orbits the sun. When the comet gets close to the sun, the sun's heat causes some of the ice to evaporate. Small pieces of rock and dust particles are set free and form a long trail behind the "head" of the comet.

The orbit of Halley's comet brings it close to Earth every 77 years or so.

About 2,200 years ago, the Chinese recorded the first sighting of the well-known Halley's Comet. This comet passes close to Earth every 77 years or so. This comet was also viewed by the Babylonians, the Greeks, and the Romans. It was last visible in 1985 and 1986.

A View of the Universe

At one time, the Chinese believed Earth was flat, or perhaps slightly curved, and floated on water. They thought the sky was a curved dome with stars fixed on its surface. They knew that the sun and moon crossed the sky at regular intervals.

About 2,200 years ago, the Chinese began to think of the universe as a giant egg. The Earth's position in this universe was similar to a yolk's position at the center of the egg. They believed the sky curved around Earth like the egg's shell.

By the year 300, they had revised their notion of the universe again. The new theory, which was called Hsüan Yeh, or "infinite empty space," claimed that the blue sky, which seems to arch overhead, was an optical illusion. Space, they said, goes on and on. By the year 800, they decided that the universe had existed for 100 million years.

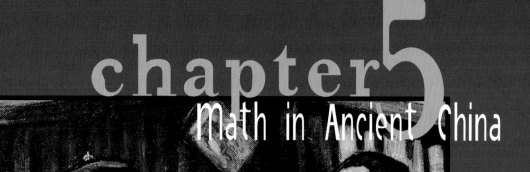

chapter 5
math in Ancient China

In ancient China, Chinese merchants used an abacus to determine how much a customer owed.

The Chinese system of numbers was developed for practical reasons more than 3,000 years ago. Alchemists needed a way to record their chemical formulas. Astronomers used math to calculate the length of the lunar month and the year. Surveyors and builders depended on math, too. They needed to measure distances and to determine the amount of materials they would need for a project.

NUMERIC SYMBOLS

Arabic	Ancient Chinese	Modern Chinese	Arabic	Ancient Chinese	Modern Chinese
1	I	一	20	=	二十
2	II	二	30	≡	三十
3	III	三	40	≣	四十
4	IIII	四	50	≣	五十
5	IIIII	五	60	⊥	六十
6	T	六	70	⊥	七十
7	∏	七	80	⊥	八十
8	∏	八	90	⊥	九十
9	∏	九	100	I	一百
10	—	十			

China's earliest system of numbers was quite simple. Each number was represented by a combination of horizontal and vertical lines. For values between one and nine, vertical lines stood for units and a horizontal line represented five units. In numbers from ten to ninety, horizontal lines stood for ten units, while a vertical line was used to represent fifty units.

Hundreds were written in the same way as units. This means that when the symbol / appeared alone, it was equal to one unit. But when / was followed by two other symbols, it represented one hundred. Similarly, thousands were written in the same way as tens. Ten thousands and millions were represented with the same symbols as units, while hundred thousands were written in the same way as tens. As a result, adjacent place values were never represented with the same set of symbols. Here's an example. The ancient Chinese would write 6,622 as follows:

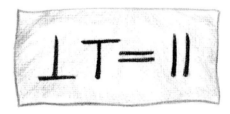

Originally, the Chinese used a blank space rather than a circle to represent none or nothing. This is how they would have written 703:

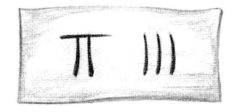

If the space was overlooked, the number would be misread as 73, rather than 703. As a result, the Chinese began using a zero symbol about 1,200 years ago.

How the Ancient Chinese Used Math

Chinese farmers determined the area of a rectangular field by multiplying its length by its width.

$$\text{length} \times \text{width} = \text{area}$$

If a field was 10 feet long and 20 feet wide, its area would be 200 square feet ($10 \times 20 = 200$).

Chinese builders calculated the volume of a pile of dirt by multiplying the length, width, and height of the pile.

$$\text{length} \times \text{width} \times \text{height} = \text{volume}$$

If a pile of dirt was 3 feet long, 4 feet wide, and 2 feet high, its volume would be 24 cubic feet ($3 \times 4 \times 2 = 24$).

Chinese mathematicians living 2,000 years ago understood the relationship between the distance across a circle—the *diameter*—and the distance around the outside edge of the circle—the *circumference.* They knew that the circumference could be determined by multiplying the diameter of a circle by a value close to 3.

By the year 200, the mathematicians knew that using the value 3.14159 would give them a more accurate answer than using just 3. Today, this mysterious value is called "pi" and represented by the Greek symbol "π."

Chinese farmers used mathematics to calculate the size of their fields. This helped them determine the value of their crop.

$$\text{circumference} = \pi d$$

Sometimes this formula is abbreviated: circumference = πd.

People in most ancient civilizations avoided using fractions, but the Chinese used them regularly. They based their calendar on a year that was 365¼ days long. They also used fractions to measure food supplies, such as grain, and to divide money among groups of people.

46

Simple Math: The Chinese Way

The ancient Chinese developed a counting rod, called an *abacus,* for addition, subtraction, multiplication, and division. Most abacuses have a wooden frame with groups of beads strung along a wooden or metal rod. Doing math with an abacus is kind of like doing math with your fingers because each bead represents a number.

Each rod is separated by a crossbar. The two beads on each rod in the compartment above the crossbar represent five units. The five beads on each rod below the crossbar represent one unit. The rod on the far right of the abacus is just like the ones column, or units column, of a large number. For example, in the number 13,458, the number 8 is in the ones column. The next rod represents the tens column (5); the third rod acts as the hundreds column (4), and so on. A number is represented by moving the appropriate beads to the crossbar. What number is represented on the abacus in the photograph below?

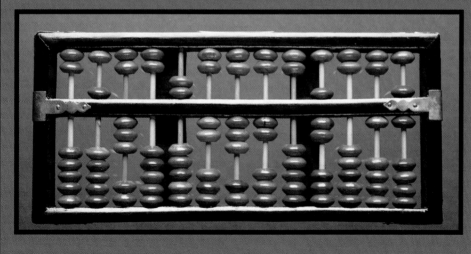

An abacus

Math and Triangles

When Chinese astronomers used gnomons to track the sun's movements over the year, the shadows they saw were always in the shape of a right triangle—a type of triangle that always has two *perpendicular* sides. Chinese surveyors and builders used right triangles to estimate the distance across rivers or swampy areas.

For example, suppose a group of builders wants to figure out the width of a mighty river. What can they do? They can use a series of pegs to create *complementary triangles.* See the illustration below.

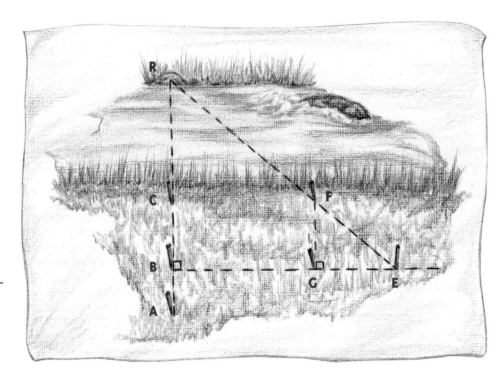

By creating complementary triangles, the Chinese could calculate the width of a river.

First, the builders drive Pegs A, B, and C into the ground on one side of the river to create a sightline to an object, such as a rock, on the opposite shore. Next, they drive another peg into the ground at point E. The imaginary line between Peg B and Peg E is perpendicular to the imaginary line between Peg B and the rock (R) on the opposite shore.

Now the builders use additional Pegs F and G to create a similar triangle on their side of the river. Since triangle EFG is complementary to the larger triangle ERB, it is possible to measure the sides of triangle EFG and use this information to calculate the distance from R to Peg B. Use the following formula.

$$RB \div EB = FG \div EG$$

This formula can be rewritten as

$$RB = (FG \times EB) \div EG.$$

If EB is 100 feet long, FG is 3 feet long, and EG is 2 feet long, then RB is 150 feet long. $[(3 \times 100) \div 2 = 300 \div 2 = 150)]$, so the river is 150 feet wide.

The rules for this form of math can be found in a Chinese book called *Nine Chapters on the Mathematical Art*. The book, which was written 2,300 years ago, also describes how to calculate the area of rectangles, triangles, and circles; how to use fractions; and how to compute the volume of cones, pyramids, and cubes. It even gives readers helpful tips for distributing grain and building walls and canals.

chapter6
Our Debt to China

Gunpowder is mixed with ingredients such as strontium, copper, and sodium to create brightly-colored fireworks.

Between 2,500 and 500 years ago, the Chinese knew more about science and technology than any other civilization in the world. Their knowledge of compasses and calendars, antiseptics and eclipses, moxa and math has had a tremendous impact on scientific advances made throughout the world during the last few centuries.

Chinese alchemy brought the world gunpowder and fireworks, brass and bronze, fine porcelain, and an amazing assortment of herbal remedies. Early Chinese healers developed medical techniques that are becoming increasingly respected and popular in North America and Europe. The Chinese healers were also the first to develop effective methods of destroying many types of disease-causing pests.

Chinese stargazers were among the first people to record sunspots and novas. They could also accurately predict comets and eclipses. When modern astronomers want to know what was happening in the skies before the year 1000, they study the Chinese records.

A German scientist purchased these items from a Chinese druggist in the early part of the twentieth century.

The basic technology used to design rockets comes from ancient China.

Space scientists also owe debt to ancient China. The rockets used to launch satellites that forecast weather and improve international communications are based on a design developed in ancient China. These same rockets powered the spacecraft that carried astronauts to the moon and the robotic spacecraft that have explored the farthest reaches of our solar system.

One of the most impressive sights in the world was built by the ancient Chinese to protect China's northern border from invaders. The Great Wall of China, the longest structure ever constructed, is nearly 4,000 miles (6,400 km) long and about 25 feet (8 m) high. Watchtowers, which are about 40 feet (12 m) tall, are spaced between 300 and 600 feet (90 and 180 m) apart.

The Great Wall of China

Construction of the Great Wall probably began about 2,400 years ago and was completed around 1600. The materials used to build this massive structure vary from place to place, depending on what was available. Some sections of the wall are made of stone and brick, while others are built from soil that was moistened and then pounded.

Many other inventions and innovations were developed in ancient China. Chinese engineers and builders constructed dams and reservoirs. They also designed irrigation systems that controlled the amount of water that reached their crops. They built canals and bridges so that food and other supplies could be transported to every corner of the vast Chinese Empire.

How China Lost Its Edge

Clearly, Chinese scientific knowledge was once far superior to that of the Europeans. But that is not true today. In the early 1600s, European science began to advance more rapidly than Chinese science. As Europe

This painting of a bridge that crosses a canal was done by a Chinese scientist named Kaku Shukei.

European astronomer Nicholas Copernicus studied ancient theories about the positions of the planets and sun. Eventually, he proposed that the sun is at the center of the solar system and that all the planets revolve around it.

entered a period called the Renaissance, Western philosophers and scientists began to study the vast knowledge accumulated by the world's most ancient cultures.

The Europeans borrowed scientific ideas from the Chinese as well as the Egyptians, Greeks, Romans, and the Mesopotamian culture. Then, they began to observe the physical, geological, and chemical properties of the world for themselves. The Europeans also asked all kinds of questions about the creatures living on Earth. The result was an explosion of scientific discovery. The spirit and excitement that arose during that time continues to inspire Western scientists today.

This renewed enthusiasm for science did not spread to China. The Chinese refused to have anything to do with ideas that came from other nations or other cultures. They distrusted foreigners and thought of Europeans as barbarians whose new ideas were inferior to the discoveries made by Chinese scientists and philosophers thousands of years ago. Because China clung to old ideas long after they were outdated, it failed to benefit from the incredible scientific and technological advances of the Industrial Revolution.

Europeans learned about China's knowledge of science in Marco Polo's *Description of the World*. The Chinese, however, had no interest in the ideas developed by other cultures.

GLOSSARY

abacus—a counting frame used in China and other countries since ancient times. The frame has columns of beads strung on wires. It can be used to rapidly add and subtract numbers and perform other mathematical calculations.

acupuncture—a form of Eastern medicine used since ancient times. It involves inserting needles into certain nerve centers (called acupuncture points) along the body to relieve pain or cure certain diseases.

alchemy—an ancient quest for knowledge through magical means, including a search for ways to extend life and turn common metals into gold.

anesthesia—loss of sensation for medical purposes.

antiseptic—a substance or process that prevents or slows down the growth of germs.

astrologer—a person who studies the stars in order to foretell future events.

astronomer—a scientist who studies stars and planets.

ch'i—the force that the ancient Chinese thought controlled blood flow through the body.

circulatory system—the organ system that carries blood through the body. It consists of the heart, the arteries, the veins, and the capillaries.

circumference—the distance around the widest part of Earth or other spherical object.

comet—a ball of ice and dust that orbits the sun.

complementary triangles—two triangles that have the same proportions, but are different in size.

constellation—a pattern of stars.

diameter—the distance across a circle.

disinfect—to destroy germs.

eclipse—a phenomenon that occurs when the moon moves between the sun and Earth (solar eclipse) or the moon is hidden by a shadow cast by the Earth as it moves between the sun and the moon (lunar eclipse).

elixir of life—a magical potion sought by alchemists to extend life or increase youthfulness.

gnomon—a vertical pole used to measure the angle of the sun by the shadow it casts.

lodestone—a rock that contains iron ore and attracts other metal objects.

lunar month—a month that is based on the moon's cycle. A lunar month is 29.530879 days long.

magnetism—a physical property that causes certain metals to be attracted to iron or steel.

magnetite—a form of iron ore that attracts other metals.

moxa (moxibustion)—an ancient Chinese medical technique in which wormwood twigs or leaves are set on fire and burn specific points along the patient's skin to relieve illness or pain.

nova—a star that suddenly increases its light output tremendously and then burns out.

perpendicular—meeting at a right angle.

pesticide—a chemical that kills pests.

porcelain—a hard, fine-grained, white ceramic that is used to make dishes, vases, and urns. It is often called china.

summer solstice—the longest day of the year in the Northern Hemisphere and the shortest day of the year in the Southern Hemisphere.

supernova—the explosion of a very large star.

Tao—in Chinese philosophy, the term means "the way" or "the path" that individuals and society as a whole should follow to achieve harmony and have a comfortable, productive life.

vaccination—to administer a preparation that protects people from a specific disease-causing agent. Most young children are vaccinated against the bacteria and viruses that cause smallpox, measles, mumps, rubella, tuberculosis, and polio.

winter solstice—the shortest day of the year in the Northern Hemisphere and the longest day of the year in the Southern Hemisphere.

yang—one of the two opposing forces that makes up the Tao. Yang is found in warm, dry, active things and in the masculine, intellectual side of individuals.

yin—one of the two opposing forces that makes up the Tao. Yin represents the cold, wet, passive side of things and the feminine, intuitive qualities of individuals.

RESOURCES

Books

Carter, Alden R. *China Past, China Future*. New York, CT: Franklin Watts, 1994.

Hoobler, Thomas. *Chinese Portraits*. Austin: Raintree/Steck Vaughn Educational Publishers, 1993.

Keeler, Stephen. *Passport to China*. New York: Franklin Watts, 1994.

McLenighan, V. *China: A History to 1949*. Chicago: Children's Press, 1983.

Prior, Katherine. *China and Southeast Asia*. Danbury, CT: Franklin Watts, 1997.

Ross, Frank Jr. *Oracle Bones, Stars, and Wheelbarrows*. Boston: Houghton Mifflin, 1990.

Temple, Robert. *The Genius of China: 3000 Years of Science, Discovery, and Invention*. New York: Simon and Schuster, 1987.

Waterlow, Julia. *The Ancient Chinese*. New York: Franklin Watts, 1994.

Internet Sites

Due to the changeable nature of the Internet, sites appear and disappear very quickly. The following resources offered useful information on ancient China at the time of publication.

Exploring Ancient World Culture includes maps, timelines, essays, and images that describe ancient civilizations in India, China, Greece, and the Near East. It can be reached at **http://eawc.evansville.edu/index.htm.**

East Middle School's Ancient Culture Page provides information about many of the world's ancient civilizations. You can learn about the ancient Greeks, Romans, Chinese, and Mayans at **http://www.macatawa.org/org/ems/anccult.html.**

Ancient World Web provides descriptions of many web sites that have information about ancient civilizations. Its address is **http://atlantic.evsc.virginia.edu/julia/AncientWorld.html.**

INDEX

ABOUT THE AUTHOR

George Beshore has written about scientific and environmental subjects for newspapers, magazines, and the federal government for more than 40 years. He has written one other book for the Science of the Past series. Mr. Beshore lives in Alexandria, Virginia with his wife, Margaret.